SEXUAL POSITIONS

GAMES LOVERS PLAY

SEXUAL POSITIONS

GAMES LOVERS PLAY

Rosie Hughes

Photography by Peter Pugh-Cook

P
PARRAGON

This is a Parragon Book

© Parragon 1997
Reprinted in 1998

Parragon
Units 13-17, Avonbridge Trading Estate,
Atlantic Road, Avonmouth,
Bristol BS11 9QD United Kingdom

Designed, produced and packaged by
Touchstone
Old Chapel Studio, Plain Road, Marden,
Tonbridge, Kent TN12 9LS United Kingdom

All pictures © Parragon

ISBN 0-75252-078-4 (hardback)
ISBN 0-75252-190-X (paperback)

Printed in Italy

DISCLAIMER
The positions and advice detailed in this book
assumes that you are a normally healthy adult.
Therefore the author, publishers, their servants
or agents cannot accept responsibility for loss or
damage suffered by individuals as a result of
attempting a position or activity referred to in
this book. It is strongly recommended that
individuals suffering from, or with a history of,
high blood pressure, heart disease or any other
medical condition, undertake demanding
physical exertion only after seeking professional
advice from their doctor.

Contents

The Strange Story of Sex

It's one of life's greatest pleasures, but many of us still carry around a burden of guilt and anxiety about it.

Sex has had a strange and chequered history. Since our first chimp-like ancestors discovered it was more fun swinging from trees together, some of the world's great brains have set themselves to embellishing the basic moves. Their names aren't recorded, but they've contributed more than most to the sum of human happiness. In these days of worldwide communication, we can choose what we like from other cultures' sex games to add to our own repertoires.

Strangest by far are the different ways human beings have treated sex. In various times and places, sex has been elevated as part of religious ceremonies or debased in devil-worship. It's been considered a civic

duty or a crime. Its most skilful practitioners have been respected as artistes or despised as sinners. Some cultures enjoy it as part of everyday life, others hedge it with taboos. It's the force that draws men and women together, yet it can be used as an assault.

It creates life, but it can carry the death penalty. And in societies where men are most obsessed with sex, women are treated like agents of the devil. Sex is part of the same life force that thrusts daisies up through concrete and makes tree roots tip buildings over. Try to repress it and it'll either burst through or continue underground – still growing, but into strange distorted shapes.

Imagine, for example, a society where children watch massacres on video but aren't allowed realistic sex education, where films can show people being disembowelled but not making love, where most young men know more about car maintenance than about their own bodies and women think the one bit of the human body that's made for nothing but pleasure is dirty …

Weird? You bet. So let's hear it for sex and love and fun – the more the merrier.

The Difference Between Men & Women

No, not the one you discovered at nursery school. The important difference between men and women is that they don't always want the same things.

OK, everyone's different and one person's thrill is another's total turn-off. But overall, just as you can say that most men are taller than most women, it's also true that most men are sexually centred on their genitals, whereas most women enjoy physical contact all over their bodies.

That's why very few men would complain if their lover unexpectedly starting fondling their penis. But the equivalent for many women feels highly unerotic, like trying to start a cold engine. Instead, they're aroused by sex play: their lovers kissing, stroking and hugging them, tangling together, enjoying the sensuous touch all over their bodies. That's why they often like making out (petting, snogging – all the fun you used to have in bus shelters or the backs of cars before you ever went all the way) more than sexual intercourse. One solution to that is to spend more time on sex play.

*Men — spend some time stroking your
lover's back, kissing, sitting with your
arms round her before you go to bed.*

❦

*And women — if you're feeling raunchy
why not surprise your lover by initiating
some hot, fast, straight-to-the-point sex?*

Another, just as important, is to listen to
each other.

Sex play is often called 'foreplay', as if it
was just a starter before the main event. In
fact, for many women it is the main event,
leading to very satisfying orgasms. Even if
they want intercourse too, sex play still has a
vital role. If men skimp on it they can be
missing out too, rushing to a climax that
would be even more powerful if they'd
taken time to build up to it.

It's even the same with oral sex. A treat
for most men, whereas some women say it
feels like being attacked by a vacuum
cleaner, if they're not in the mood. Women
often need to feel aroused first, and that
may take longer than men expect.

Does this have to be a big problem?
No, as long as you're aware of your lover's
needs and preferences. If you've always
thought of sex as being something to do
with just one part of your body, try some
sensuous all-body techniques. The skin is
full of pleasure-receptors just waiting to be
awakened. You'll discover a wealth of new
erogenous zones.

Exploring His Body

Men's bodies aren't admired or displayed as often as women's are. Apart from the odd rather self-conscious pin-up, we don't often see a male body shown for its beauty. But why should men's bodies be neglected?

When you're both feeling lazily relaxed, take time to discover your lover's body. Start by running your fingers lightly down his belly and into his pubic hair, continuing by stroking his penis.

You can take your time around here, as most men love being played with like this. The most sensitive parts of his body are his penis, especially the tip (from the ridge to the end) and the testicles, which he will love to be stroked or gently cradled. He may like his penis held and rubbed or squeezed quite firmly, but never try this with his testicles – it's agonising. A circumcised penis may be less sensitive, though this may provide more staying power and help to delay his orgasm.

Gently pull back his foreskin – the loose skin that slides over the top of the penis – unless he's been circumcised, in which case the foreskin has been removed and the end is smooth and uncovered. Lick your fingers before you touch up here if he finds a dry touch uncomfortable. Below the

tip of his penis, or 'helmet', is a ridge that's particularly noticeable if he's circumcised.

Both men and women have a highly sensitive area of skin called the perineum between the genital area and the anus (the arsehole or asshole, depending if you're British or American), so don't forget to stroke that too. Many men like you to press or stroke their perineum if you can reach while making love.

Men tend to like their penis held firmly and rubbed quite hard, especially the closer they come to orgasm. Their balls, on the other hand, are terribly easy to hurt, so always touch them lightly. Continue this loving, arousing touch by running your fingertips over his whole body, varying the pressure from featherlight to squeezes.

CALL ME NAMES

Sex has inspired a whole language of its own, sometimes medical-sounding, sometimes romantic or poetic, often earthy.

Most people know dozens of friendly names for a man's penis, the part he puts inside a woman: cock, willy, shlong, dick, knob, prick and dozens more reflect the down-to-earth relationship men have with this part of their body.

His testicles – the sex organs where sperm is produced, hanging just behind the penis – are called balls or nuts or bollocks except when people use expressions like 'love orbs' as a joke.

Exploring Her Body

Make this journey of discovery on a long evening or a Sunday morning when there's no rush to do anything. Then you can take all the time in the world to discover new routes to ecstasy.

Women are sometimes quite shy about their bodies generally, especially the genital area which they think is particularly ugly. They don't have as many friendly names for their genitals as men do. Pussy, fanny, muff and quim are used for both the vulva, which means pretty much all the genital area you could see if it wasn't hidden by pubic hair, and the vagina, which is internal – the passage leading from the vulva to the womb.

Confusingly the British often call this whole area the fanny, which is what Americans call their bottoms. Cunt should be a perfectly good everyday word for this much loved area – too bad it's commonly used as an insult.

A couple of inches inside the vagina, at the front, there may or may not be the Grafenberg Spot or G-spot, a source of intense pleasure for many women. Try stroking inside with a well lubricated finger, pressing gently upwards (towards her abdomen, not inwards towards her womb): bliss for some women, but it doesn't do anything for others. So maybe the G-spot is just a bonus that we don't all have, like high cheekbones or an ability to read maps!

Then there's the clitoris, the wonderful little button near the top of the vulva that has no purpose other than sexual pleasure. It's usually just called the clit, though a friend of mine very accurately calls it her Magic Come-Button. But women often need to feel aroused before they like having their clitoris touched – otherwise it may be too sensitive and just hurt. Even if she likes it rubbed quite firmly when she's close to orgasm, it may be delicate at other times.

Women often prefer you to rub around rather than on it. It's worth getting to know a woman's individual ways, so that love-making becomes more reliably rewarding.

Around all this are two sets of labia – or lips to those of us who don't speak Latin in everyday life. The inner lips are the frilly folds around the vulva (often big enough to show through the pubic hair) and the outer lips are where the hair grows.

Enjoy discovering this area, and your lover's individual responses to your touch, as part of a tour of her whole body. People have the most versatile erogenous zones – for some it's the inside of their elbows, while others get a tingle down their spine if you run your fingers down the back of their neck. Pressing the lowest part of the stomach, just above the pubic bone, reaches a very sexy spot for lots of people. Take time to run your fingers lightly over her skin and discover how many erotic touches there are.

Sexual Adventures

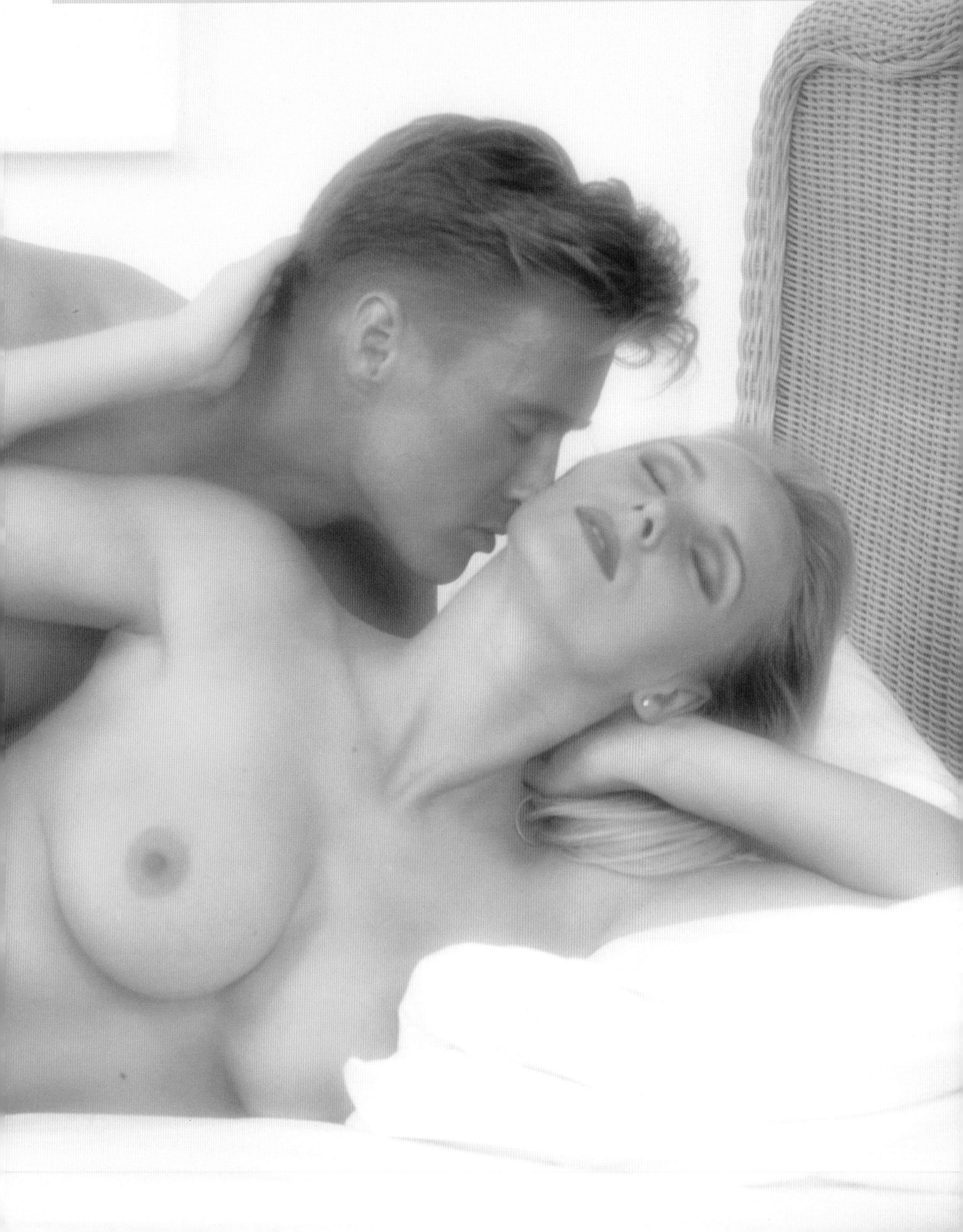

Breathing Your Lover In

Kneeling facing each other is a beautiful way to start making love, when you have time for a slow build-up of arousal leading to a passionate climax.

For an unusually sensuous start to love-making, undress and kneel up, facing each other. If you like, you can spread a little massage oil up the front of your body and thighs – not letting your lover touch you just yet. Place one hand on your lover's chest and the other on their stomach. Feel the movement of their breathing.

Try to breathe fully in, so that your stomach expands rather than your chest: your partner will be able to tell you if this is happening. You don't have to breathe unnaturally slowly or deeply – in fact, you'll start feeling dizzy if you do – but just let the

TAKE YOUR TIME

As the minutes pass, start letting your bodies move together, skin sliding past skin until you can't stop yourselves making love any longer.

⤜

You can stay with this position, the woman lifting up a bit so the man can enter her then settling down either on her knees — on a cushion if she needs the extra height — or with her legs around his waist.

⤜

Or lie on the floor together. But the longer you make this last, the more intensely you're likely to climax.

breath enter your body fully. This is, incidentally, how we're meant to breathe all the time, to be fully grounded and energetic. Then start trying to breathe in rhythm with each other, each adjusting the tempo gradually to meet the other.

Imagine sexual energy starting to move in your groin with each breath, gradually expanding to flow through your body.

Now move closer together so you feel your lover's breath moving with your own body, your bellies pressing together as you breathe in and your breaths mingling in the air around your faces as you breathe out. Stay pressed close together.

Imagine that your lover's essence spreads into the air around them and you are breathing it in, blending together. Try not to move at this stage: just concentrate on feeling the warmth of your lover's body and the rise and fall of their breath in time with yours. Imagine your lover's essence and your own mingling on your breath and entering each other's bodies.

Gradually start stroking each other's backs, arms and buttocks very slowly, still breathing in harmony. Soon your breath may start to quicken as you become aroused, but try to keep it in pace with the slower one as long as possible.

Classic Missionaries

The classic position is lying face to face, man on top between the woman's legs. It allows for a lot of body contact, kissing, looking at each other and freedom to stroke and embrace.

Some things pass the test of time, and the missionary position has to be one of them. It's a classic – relaxed, comfortable and affectionate, inviting you to put your arms round each other.

Its rather strait-laced associations come from tales that Christian missionaries ordered happy native islanders to stop their other sex games and do it this way only. You wouldn't want this to be the only dish on the menu. But it's a lot more fun than its reputation suggests.

There are all kinds of variations on the basic theme. A woman can push her legs wider apart or wrap them round the man's waist. If she's very flexible she can rest her feet on the man's shoulders, while he takes care not to put too much weight on them. Leaning on them very gently, or letting her push against his shoulders, will raise her buttocks, pressing them against him and slightly changing the angle of entry.

She can also try changing the angle by putting pillows under her bottom, as many as she finds comfortable. This can be helpful for another variation, in which she puts her legs together while he lies astride or on top of her. It may take several attempts to get in this way, but it lets the woman hold his penis tight between her thighs.

Many women love the missionary position, especially when they're feeling lazy and relaxed.

Oddly, even the most independent women may be quite passive in bed, and secretly enjoy the feeling of being 'done to' rather than doing.

Others hate it, feeling squashed and restricted. But a woman can play an active role too, by squeezing with her vagina, caressing his back and shoulders, running her fingernails over her skin or slipping her hand down, if there's room, to stroke his groin.

RIDING HIGH

There was a lot of excitement a few years ago when the 'riding high' position — also known as coital alignment technique or CAT — was rediscovered as a way for many women to reach orgasm through intercourse alone.

Start as if for the missionary position, then the man shuffles slightly higher up the woman's body, so his penis enters her at a different angle.

Stay very close to each other, for a rocking movement rather than deep thrusts. It's a completely different feel and, once you get used to the movement, can be profoundly satisfying.

Women On Top

Changing places can be fun for both partners. This has given many women their first orgasms – helpful for the man too, since he's finding out how best to please her.

If you're used to the missionary position it may feel funny the first time you try it reversed, with the woman on top. This way round, the woman does most of the work while the man takes a rest. It's easiest if she squats on top of him or kneels astride. That way she can let his penis slip in and out by lifting her hips, changing the speed and rhythm as much as she wants.

When she's settled into this rhythm, she can lean forward to lie on him like a frog, still with her legs drawn up so she can keep the movement going. She could also turn round and face his feet, changing the sensation for both of them.

It's more of a challenge to try this with the woman lying flat on top. She'll probably have to hold onto him and maybe anchor her feet round his ankles to get any movement. If they prefer, the man can take the lead by holding her hips and thrusting powerfully from underneath.

For a woman, being on top can feel delightfully powerful, with the chance of controlling speed and movement. If she's easy-going in everyday life, this position is a way of exploring her more assertive side.

A man too can enjoy a break from doing all the work on top – though, if both partners like, he can still control the movement from below, and he will love to see his woman's breasts swinging and bouncing above him, reaching up to cup them in his hands or catching them in his mouth as she leans down over him. Her pussy is in easy reach for him to play with too, and her ecstatic writhings will increase his pleasure.

The X-Factor

Changing the angle stimulates different parts of both of you, as the pleasure zone slides all around him and inside her.

Sitting on top of her man, facing him, holding his penis inside her with one hand, an agile woman can bring her feet forward so they're beside his face – both on the same side. She then leans slowly backwards till her shoulders are lying on the bed on the other side of his legs.

In other words, they're now making an X-shape, with the woman probably arching her back to try to keep his penis inside. In this position it's pressing against the front of her vagina, which may stimulate her G-spot.

Feel the changing sensations as you make an X in other positions too. Face each other or both face the same way; man or woman on top or side by side. You can both stretch your legs out and it is useful to have a big bed or plenty of floor space. Or try in an interlaced position, each with one leg between the other's.

Side By Side

You can share the pleasure of looking at your lover and deeply kissing from a number of different angles.

Face-to-face positions are popular with lovers because they allow so much activity by both partners, pressing and tangling with their whole bodies as well as kissing and looking at each other. But it doesn't have to be the classic missionary.

A very affectionate variation is to lie side by side, facing each other. Even better, one of you puts your top leg over the other's thigh or waist, holding the two of you warmly together. This gives a feeling of wide-open genital contact, also leaving room to reach round and help the penis in or fondle your lover. This is an easy-going position for sex, cuddling or falling asleep together.

You could also try wrapping your legs around your lover's waist, as long as the bed is soft enough or your partner light enough not to crush your thigh – this is where waterbeds come into their own. Or lie with your legs stretched out pressing against each other – this restricts movement a bit but allows the woman to hold his penis between her thighs.

WHY TRY DIFFERENT POSITIONS?

If you're both perfectly happy with one favourite way of making love, that's just fine. But trying some different ways opens up new possibilities for enjoyment. There's a technical and a psychological reason for trying a new position.

Changing the angle of entry stimulates slightly different parts of both penis and vagina, and may allow more overall genital contact. It may allow deeper or more shallow penetration.

Some positions allow more room to manoeuvre or let you caress different parts of your lover's body. And there's the fun of trying something new, especially if it has a slightly daring edge to it.

Doggy-Style

This one has a risqué feel to it, even though it's probably the oldest way to enjoy sex and is how many of us first saw sex being enjoyed, even if we didn't realize what our neighbours' pets were up to. Perhaps because of this it has a raunchy, slightly illicit feel.

Just as the name suggests, the woman kneels on all fours and the man enters her vagina from behind. One of them may have to guide his penis in. She can change the angle by lifting or lowering her shoulders; the more her spine slopes down towards her head, the more her pussy can press against the man's balls and the easier it is for him to stay inside her. In this position she can also hook her feet around his thighs to hold him close to her.

The man can reach around her thigh to fondle her or lean forward to hold her breasts, though he may also enjoy watching them bouncing rhythmically as he thrusts into her. Pillows are handy here – and a well-padded headboard – to stop her bumping her head on the wall with each enthusiastic thrust.

The woman can also lie on her face with her legs wide apart, lifting her buttocks high so she can guide the man in.

Ducks & Donkeys

Entering from behind gives the man a chance to hold his lover's breasts and feel her butt pressing against him. Women too can play an active role.

Some women dislike rear-entry positions, perhaps because of a belief that sex is depersonalized if you can't see each other's faces. That's a pity because there are so many possible variations, from the raunchy to the lovingly intimate.

In a position known as the Donkey, the woman stands, bending forward with legs parted so her man can enjoy the sight of her vulva and butt before he enjoys the feel of them. It's one of those positions that clothes make even better – men love a woman doing this wearing nothing but a short skirt.

Or she may lie across the bed or some other piece of furniture comfortable enough to lie on, with her pussy just at the edge of it, while he stand or kneels to enter her from behind. Another one that feeds his

It's good to talk but it's even better to talk and listen. Be aware of body language – your lover may be trying to tell you they don't like some technique or some part of their body being touched.

❧

Whether the unease is caused by a sports injury or a sexual hang-up, ignoring their wishes will make them feel invaded. This causes tension – a major turn-off. If they feel safe that you'll only do what they want, they will enjoy the experience and eventually loosen up.

fantasies of creeping up and taking her by surprise. In fact, rear-entry positions feed many women's fantasies too.

Loving a person can somehow dampen your sexual fantasies about them, as if you ought to show them more respect. But sex is a time to liberate your imagination – not seeing their lover's face can free people to revel in their fantasies. So a faceless Mystery Man holding his woman from behind may be startled at how erotically she responds.

But one of the most affectionate gestures between two lovers is curling up together like two spoons. This wonderfully adaptable position lends itself as much to falling asleep still stuck together as it does to passionate lovemaking. His arms around her stroke her belly or cup her breasts as he thrusts into her. She can join in by pressing her buttocks against him, gyrating and squeezing his penis, stretching back to dig her fingers into his butt and thighs or reaching down to stroke his balls and hold his penis.

Then, all passion spent, they can fall asleep without moving, his penis still warmly inside her as they drift off to sleep. Nothing is more reassuring than falling asleep with your arms around your lover, or theirs around you, from behind, buttocks pressed intimately to stomach. In fact, the Chinese call this sexual position Mandarin Ducks Entwined – mandarin ducks being the Chinese symbol of faithful married love.

Sideways On

A lazy, relaxed position, ideal for steamy nights under a slow-moving ceiling fan.

Try this for dreamy, relaxed love-making when the night's too hot for pressing together. Think of a woman sitting sideways on a man's lap – her shoulder towards his face – with one arm round his shoulders and his arms around her.

It's exactly this position but lying down, she on her back with her legs over his thighs, he on his side. Or vary it by both stretching out full length, just meeting in the middle like an X. She can lift her legs in the air for a sensuous feeling of abandonment.

You can still reach out and run your fingertips or nails along the contours of your lover's body.

COMING TOGETHER

Ejaculating is deeply relaxing for most men. But some women can have a whole string of orgasms lasting several minutes.

Or you may find yourself carried on a long slow wave of pleasure that never quite breaks and finishes by gently ebbing away. This is frustrating if you're desperately pushing for an orgasm that won't quite happen, so let yourself float along with it and enjoy the prolonged pleasure it gives.

Incidentally, it's rare for both partners to come at the same time. Explosive though it may be if it happens, don't put a lot of effort into trying for it – sex doesn't work like synchronised swimming. Women often reach orgasm through 'foreplay' or sex play, then enjoy intercourse either for a second orgasm or as a kind of 'afterplay' while the man reaches his climax.

If you can summon up enough will-power, try a different kind of orgasm for a change: Stop moving just before you come and imagine the sexual energy flooding into every atom of your body. This could result in a long, deep climax that seems to spread through your whole body.

PILLOW TALK

Why does sex send men off to sleep faster than women, who then lie there feeling lonely? Men can't altogether help it – it's just a physical reaction caused by ejaculating.

But a smart man will keep himself awake long enough to kiss, cuddle and maybe talk for a while. Good sex creates a relaxing after-glow that both partners can enjoy – and enjoying it together helps build warmth and trust that lead to a happier sex life.

Interlacing

Making love is easiest and most obvious with the woman's legs around the man, or sometimes with his legs outside hers. But there are several positions with legs interlaced, each lover putting a leg between the other's thighs.

Interlacing gives both partners plenty of opportunity for pressing against their lover's thigh for some beautifully diffused stimulation.

One version is like the sideways-on position but more tangled together – lying on his side beside the woman who's on her back, the man puts his top leg between her thighs, his knee resting on her far thigh. Her nearest leg is bent over his, her far leg is stretched out. Try it, it's a lot less complicated than it sounds.

You can work out a number of variations on this basic theme, with the woman lying half-facing or half-turned away from the man – either partner on top, or side by side, with one of her legs straight and one around him. One variation often leads naturally into another.

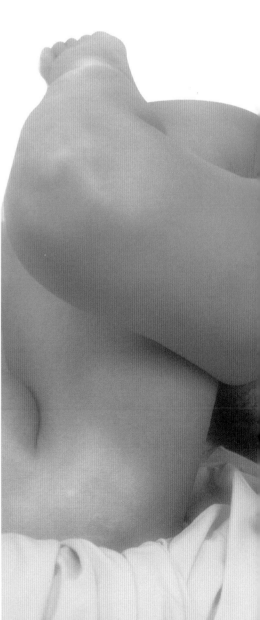

THE SQUEEZE

One of the best sex secrets a woman can learn is to tighten the grip of her vagina. It's a simple exercise — try to stop peeing in mid-flow. You'll be exercising the same pelvic floor muscles that hold your man's penis when he's inside you. Once you've got the hang of it you can do a few squeezes anywhere, any time, holding the muscles tight for about 10 seconds before releasing, then repeating for a few minutes.

It adds to your enjoyment as well as his, when you grip him tight or rhythmically squeeze and release as he thrusts, opening up to let him into you and squeezing as he pulls back.

This is an especially useful exercise for women who have had children or whose man is small.

Standing

When people describe something other than sex as 'the most fun you can have standing up' they're forgetting you don't have to lie down to make love.

Standing positions remind us of our teenage forays along the sexual borderlands, making out in doorways and secret places when we had a chance. There's a hint of the taboo, of not being respectably in bed, of breaking the rules – which of course adds to the pleasure.

Doorways are actually a very good place for standing sex, since you're most likely to find a doorstep there. And unless you both have the same length legs, a step of some sort helps a lot. If there's not much difference in height she can give him an added treat by wearing high heels to make up a few extra inches.

She can wind one leg around his waist, or both legs, if his back and her legs are strong enough to hold her and she's agile enough to cling with her legs while sliding up and down his penis. Cheating just a bit, she can sit on the edge of a table or even a window-sill for a similar effect.

If she faces away from him, this position has an even rougher edge, leading to a fast, wild climax.

Given the illicit aura of standing sex in the Western world, it's funny to think it has received the highest accolade of respectability – it's one of the sexual positions shown in sacred Indian temple carvings, a reminder of a time and place in which people understood sexual pleasure was a gift from the gods.

Face to face or rear entry standing positions are ideal for 'quickie' sex, with raw urgency and breathless energy.

Ideal for partially clothed sex with an illicit feel, adding to the excitement and visual stimulation.

Sitting

A chance for easy, relaxed sex or wild lovemaking, with erotic memories of times when you enjoyed the journey all the more because you couldn't go all the way.

Seated positions create a different aura again. Not quite as rough-and-ready as standing, they still have an element of making out and doing it in an unusual place. A reminder of feeling each other up in the cinema or while baby-sitting, never daring to go all the way. Here, of course, you can. But keep the memory in your mind of that burning, erotic longing you used to feel.

Use this as a chance for lots of sex play before you get your clothes off, to recreate the intensity of those times.

Deep armchairs offer a plushy, luxurious arena for sex games, though a wooden

kitchen chair is easier to manoeuvre on and more supportive. Vanishing into a deeply sprung seat is frustrating when a man is trying to achieve some kind of movement inside his lover, so you may have to be inventive – she can help by wedging her feet against the sides of the chair or wrapping her legs around him and pushing backwards and forwards.

The most usual positions have the woman sitting on the man's lap, whether sideways, facing or with her back to him.

But if the chair's comfortable enough he could sit astride her for a change.

A rocking chair or swing add an interesting extra element, though you may have less control over your movement when the chair's joining in.

Inversion

A rush of blood to the brain heightens the pleasure of lovemaking, adding a heady sense of wildness.

Remember doing a 'wheelbarrow' when you were little – you walking along on your hands while a friend held your feet at waist-level? The grown-up version has the man standing and the woman clinging round his waist with her legs. It's easiest if she starts by sitting on his lap, facing away from him, and arching her back to help him get his penis inside. Then she can slide forward while he carefully rises to his feet, holding her hips.

If she's top of her yoga class, try this one face to face, holding each other as she leans slowly backwards to put her hands on the floor, her legs wrapped around his waist. This can be mind-blowing for her man as he watches her hair flow back, her breasts lifting and sliding.

Either partner can lie with their head hanging over the edge of the bed while making love. And a beautifully connected version involves facing each other while

sitting across a single bed or a bit of armless furniture such as a pouffe. He slips inside her, then both partners lean back, legs around each other or his legs down and hers around his waist, till they have their heads as near the floor as they want.

Or she can sit on his lap on a chair – facing either way – and slide her head slowly towards the floor, gripping tightly with her vagina to hold him inside her, while he supports her with his legs. A pile of cushions on the floor makes this easier, and she can push some away if she wants .

Why try these upside-down variations? Because the dizzying effect of blood rushing to your head can add to the build-up of excitement as you make love. The element of danger adds to the psychological buzz.

Obviously, stop at once if it's not feeling good or if you start to feel uncomfortable – and watch out for signs of this in your partner. But as long as you're not being held down, and you have a panic signal for if you need to get up quickly (see page 74) you can enjoy the dizzy thrill of an upside-down orgasm.

Please don't even try this if you have high blood pressure or heart trouble.

Whole Body Pleasure

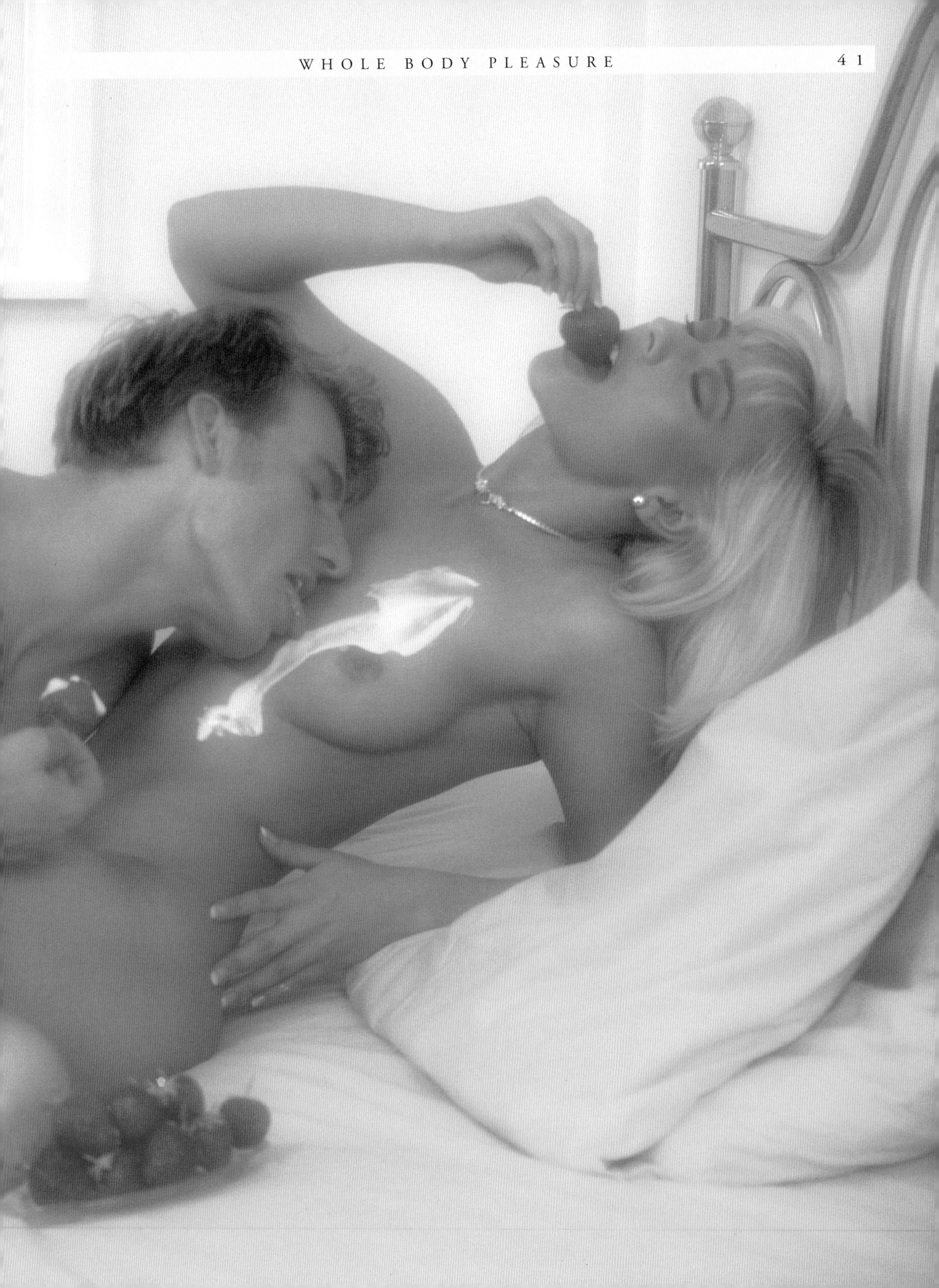

Fire Under The Skin

It's time women shared the big sex secret with men – that the whole body is an erogenous zone.

Anyone who has ever felt waves still rippling through their arms and legs after a spectacular climax knows that pleasure isn't just located in one small part of the body. Yet all too often we act as if there's a starter motor between our partner's legs and dive straight on to it. The resulting thrill is often brief and localized.

We all tend to think sex is mainly about penis and vagina, with testicles and clitoris as the boundaries and maybe nipples as the one distant outpost. But this means both men and women are missing out on a major source of pleasure – one that offers so much variety that you need never get bored. Why waste about 95 per cent of the skin's surface, which – in both men and women – is all packed with nerve endings just waiting to be set alight?

It's an easy enough mistake to make. We were all brought up feeling faintly – or not so faintly – embarrassed about our

Arouse your lover, and yourself, with light touches that are enough to excite but not to satisfy. Trace the length of their body with your fingertips, following all their contours along the way.

Do the same with your fingernails — your lover will notice how different it feels if you pull them lightly towards you or trail them in the opposite direction. Blow onto exposed skin. Tickle with your tongue. Rub scented oil into each other. Above all, take time for unhurried pleasure.

bodies' capacity for pleasure, and many girls manage to forget it altogether. Boys find it difficult to ignore the wonderful toy that's attached to them but girls may regard 'down there' as forbidden territory.

All kinds of girly entertainments lead to the dawning discovery that skin feels … mmmm, good. The movement of her scalp as a friend does her hair, thighs squeezing a trotting horse, scented water flowing over her stomach in an hour-long bath, needles of cold water under the shower, body lotion smoothed languorously on to her arms. What boys gain on the merry-go-rounds, girls gain on the swings.

Then you're grown up and you can put it all together — men's unselfconscious pleasure in genital sex, women's sensuality spreading through the whole body. Each offers its own pleasures. Together they're magic.

Fellatio

On a special night, give your man the treat of his dreams.
Nothing else you do will please him so much.

Oral sex is many men's favourite game apart from sexual intercourse. It's not a substitute, but it gives a sharp, intensely focused orgasm that's not about love or intimacy or anything – just pure sex. Sometimes that's exactly what a man needs.

The most straightforward technique is for the woman to put her man's penis in her mouth and move her head backwards and forwards – or up and down, depending on their position – being careful to keep it away from her teeth. It's an advanced skill, so she'd better go slowly at first.

Variations include flicking the ridge with her tongue, licking his balls, sucking just the end of his penis quite hard and pulling her head back so it pops out,

It can be quite difficult to stretch your lips around an erect penis while keeping your teeth away from it. The choke reflex can be uncontrollable when something big is in your mouth – if this happens the man should stay still so the woman can control the level of penetration.

running her tongue around the ridge and
very gently holding one testicle in her
mouth for a moment. She can combine
hand and mouth movements, perhaps
holding the shaft of his penis and sucking
the end while cradling his balls.

   Pulling back all the loose skin
of his penis towards the root,
so the penis looks stiff and
tight, can feel better for
him and be easier than
coping with the skin
moving in her mouth,
blunting her suction.

Cunnilingus and 69

A taste of honey, a touch that turns skin into electricity.
This is one of a lover's most skilful secrets.

Most lovers enjoy cunnilingus, even if they're cautious to start off with. Every skilled lover is glad of a trick that can so easily please his woman and he will enjoy the natural perfume of her body, including the special scent of her pussy when she's warm and aroused.

Oral sex is easier to perform on a woman than a man, given the small and unobtrusive shape of her vulva. But the same trait can cause problems, since it's nowhere near so obvious what to do or where.

To start with a man can gently part his lover's labia, without stretching the skin, and run his tongue flat from the slit of her vaginal opening up over her clitoris. As she becomes more aroused the clitoris will swell and harden and may become too sensitive to touch, so she'll prefer him to lick around it.

As when she's doing it to him, gentle movements with a well wetted tongue can hardly go wrong. Vary movements with the tongue flat and pointed, occasionally thrusting into her vagina.

Impending orgasm can make one partner lose track of what they're doing at what may be a crucial moment for the other. But with good nature you can overlook this in favour of the raunchy satisfaction you'll both gain as you continue. For sheer sweaty sexy sex, 69 is hard to beat.

WHAT'S YOUR FAVOURITE NUMBER?

Sixty-nine is a winner for both sexes.
You can do this from any position, lying side by side, with one or the other partner crouching on top or even standing with the woman upside-down for a while if the man's strong enough.

❧

Some couples like one or other lying flat on top, though if this is the man he needs to keep checking she's still comfortable.
(See 'Pressing the Panic Button' page 74.)

Other Places

Explore the varied pleasures of your lover's body, discovering the intricate sensuality of a tender and erotic touch.

*M*aking love with your hands is not a poor substitute for the 'real thing'. Touching, stroking, squeezing and kneading are all part of the lover's repertoire. Being brought to orgasm with skilful hand techniques can be more erotically satisfying than sexual intercourse, especially for women, since so much of their pleasure comes from outside the vagina.

For men too it's a different kind of orgasm with advantages of its own. In general, men like stronger pressure and more vigorous movement than women, at least to start with. Men become so sensitive the moment they've come that they can't bear you to touch any part of their penis for a few minutes afterwards.

Women often like firmer pressure and faster rubbing as they get closer to a climax, and may want the movement to continue for a while as the orgasm flows through them. But the important thing is to find out by experience what works for you and your lover.

Men can also reach orgasm with other parts of their lover's body – between her breasts is a favourite place, as she squeezes them together with her hands. Many men like their penis held between her thighs or buttocks, pressed into her armpit or even held between the soles of her feet.

Both sexes can reach a climax rubbing against their lover's thigh when it's pushed between their own thighs. Be careful not to knee him in the balls, a horribly painful turn-off. But for women in particular, rhythmically moving against a lover's thigh provides a wonderfully diffused pressure to the clitoris and the whole vulva area, leading to a slow and intense orgasm.

International Relations

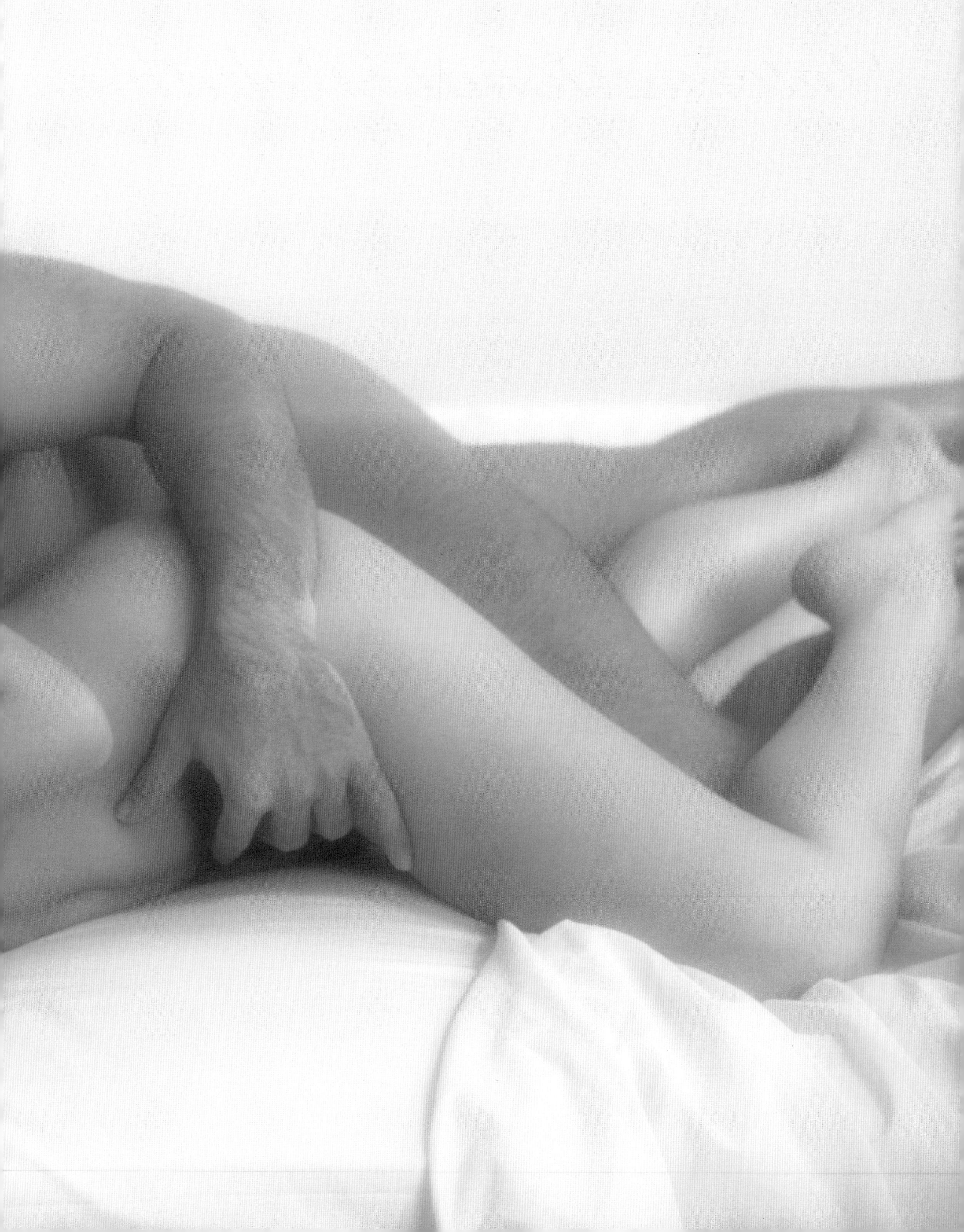

The Kama Sutra

Reminders of a time and place in which love was sacred and sex was a ritual of worship. Some positions help the woman open up as widely as possible so entry is easy.

The most famous lovers' manual in the world, the Kama Sutra was written in India nearly two thousand years ago. It's about love and relationships, with sexual skills playing an accepted part of a full and happy life.

The Kama Sutra concentrates on all aspects of lovemaking, not just sexual intercourse and the variety of positions available to lovers. It talks a lot about kissing, fondling and sex play – and says accomplished lovers never hurry these.

Though it's best known now for its variety of sexual positions, it describes just as many ways to embrace and to kiss – from gently brushing lips, to the man kissing the woman's upper lip while she kisses his lower lip, to Tongue Fighting with mouths clasped together and tongues exploring.

One of the most famous Kama Sutra positions is the Spinning Top, in which the man lies on his back or sits leaning back while the woman climbs on top of him. With him inside her, she then swivels in a

THE SLIPPERY STAND-BY
Lubricating jelly is a useful standby if a woman's vagina isn't moist enough for comfortable sex. Use one that's specifically for this purpose, because it won't damage a condom.

The vagina becomes naturally damp and slippery when a woman is sexually aroused, so if it's not happening it usually means she's not ready. Men are quicker off the mark than women, but it's worth being patient and helping her catch up — it'll mean a longer and more satisfying experience for both of you.

circle. He can help by holding her waist or hips and turning her.

For the Swing, they start in the same position but she sits with her back to him, rocking backwards and forwards with her feet on the floor for leverage.

In the Yawning Position she sits on his lap, facing him, with her hands and feet on his shoulders. Then she can lift herself towards him or stretch her feet back behind his head as she leans backwards. This position is easier than it may at first appear.

In the Widely Open position, the lovers face each other. The woman lies back with her spine arched as high as possible, supporting her weight on her feet and shoulders, while the man kneels or squats between her legs.

If she's very flexible, she can try the Position of the Wife of Indra, lying back with her knees drawn up so that the man presses her thighs against her body as he lies on top of her. If he's heavy or she's not acrobatic, she could just raise her knees beside him and pull her thighs as far back as she finds comfortable with her hands.

For a Kama Sutra fantasy, wear bangles and necklaces and let the sound they make as you move be a counterpoint to your own cries and sighs.

Chinese Fireworks

Thousands of years of civilization gave the Chinese time to perfect the art of erotic pleasure. When 'jade stem' plays with 'jade gate', the senses explode.

As in all sensuous traditions, the ancient Chinese taught that sex was a skill to be savoured and unhurried, with a lot more happening than just sexual intercourse. When the poet Huang O invited her lover to 'play with the lotus blossom under my green jacket' you can bet she was thinking of something long and slow.

China's traditional Taoist teachings describe different kinds and patterns of movement, for example a rhythm of three or nine shallow thrusts to one deep, since a variation in the rhythm prevents either partner becoming bored. Try the nine different kinds of thrusts, including fast 'like

*Try 'Autumn Dog' for sheer
athleticism — man and woman squat back to back, supporting
themselves on hands and feet; man lowers his head and using his
hand manages to get his jade stem into her jade gate. But don't be
disappointed if this ends in helpless laughter rather than orgasm.*

a snake entering a hole to hibernate' or a mixture of deep and teasingly shallow but alternating quickly 'as a sparrow picking the leftovers of rice in a mortar'. Or 'poise, then strike like an eagle catching an elusive hare'.

The Chinese culture is highly poetic, so it's not surprising that erotic discourse has its own evocative language. Jade was a symbol of all that's most precious and beautiful, hence expressions like his 'jade stem' or 'jade peak' and her 'jade gate'. In the position known as Late Spring Donkey she bends forward to stand on hands and feet and he enters from behind holding her waist. For Dark Cicada Clings to a Branch she lies on her stomach with legs wide, as he holds her shoulders and enters from behind. A Phoenix Plays in a Red Cave is the name given to a variation of the missionary position where she raises her legs and holds her feet up in the air.

*Traditional Chinese teachings
recommend every kind of sex play, to
delay ejaculation and lead to serial
orgasms for the woman The man
conserves his 'life force' and prolongs
the pleasure for both of them.*

Japanese Style

Behind the paper screens is a world of eroticism where elegant formality blends with an earthy appreciation of the senses.

Travellers to Japan over the centuries have been startled at the variety of sex aids openly available in this intensely formal society. But why not? An active and even demanding sexuality has always been part of their culture, for women as much as for men. For a Japanese sex game, you could start very slowly and formally, almost ritually. The woman can pile her hair on top of her head with hairpins – since the nape

of a woman's neck is highly erotic in Japanese lore. He can brush her nape with his lips or lick it very lightly and teasingly. Japanese lovers are frequently shown still clothed, so keep your kimonos on and enjoy the feeling of skin against silk or brocade.

Squatting positions are a favourite. He sits on his heels behind her, his hands hidden under her rumpled kimono, and she squats on his lap, her head thrown back beside his or forward to support herself on her hands. The soft movement of her hair as it starts slipping down adds to the erotic ambiance – as it has done in every culture where women normally wear their hair neatly pinned up.

Heighten the intensity by whispering or communicating only by touch. Japanese lovers are traditionally quiet. In small wooden houses with paper screens instead of inner walls, lovers try not to intrude on other people with noise – old Japanese prints show women stuffing their lustrous long hair into their mouths to silence themselves at the moment of orgasm.

French Fancy

Recreate some turn-of-the-century decadence with fans and feathers and gilded mirrors.

The French were having a wild time 100 years ago, by all accounts. It was a period of sexual liberation, of 'gai Paris', of pleasure domes ornate with gilt and mirrors and ostrich feather fans. As with all cultures – or myths – we can take what we choose to play with. So forget about harsh reality and imagine a playground of sensuality. Put some mirrors around the room and spin a fantasy of uninhibited sexual pleasure.

If you have a featherlike fan, get your lover to lie still while you run it lightly over their skin. Position the mirrors so you see both your faces as you near orgasm.

One brothel game of the time involved onlookers blind-folding a man and woman and tying their hands behind their back, then cheering them on as they found inventive ways of making love without using either their sight or their hands.

Try this at home, but make sure you've looped your wrists with something easily slipped off, since there won't be anyone to release you. The joy of this game is that it brings the whole body into play.

The blindfold is very important too, since skin becomes more erotically sensitive than ever when you can't use your most dominant sense, that of sight.

Travelling in France must have had some unexpected rewards, since there's a very energetic position known as the Lyons Stagecoach. The man lies on his back with the woman sitting on top, her feet either beside his chest or past his shoulders, supporting herself with her hands or leaning forward. She then bounces up and down as if in a coach thundering along a bumpy road. Take some time to get a rhythm going before you leap too energetically, though, or it could be bruisingly painful for your man.

Games Lovers Play

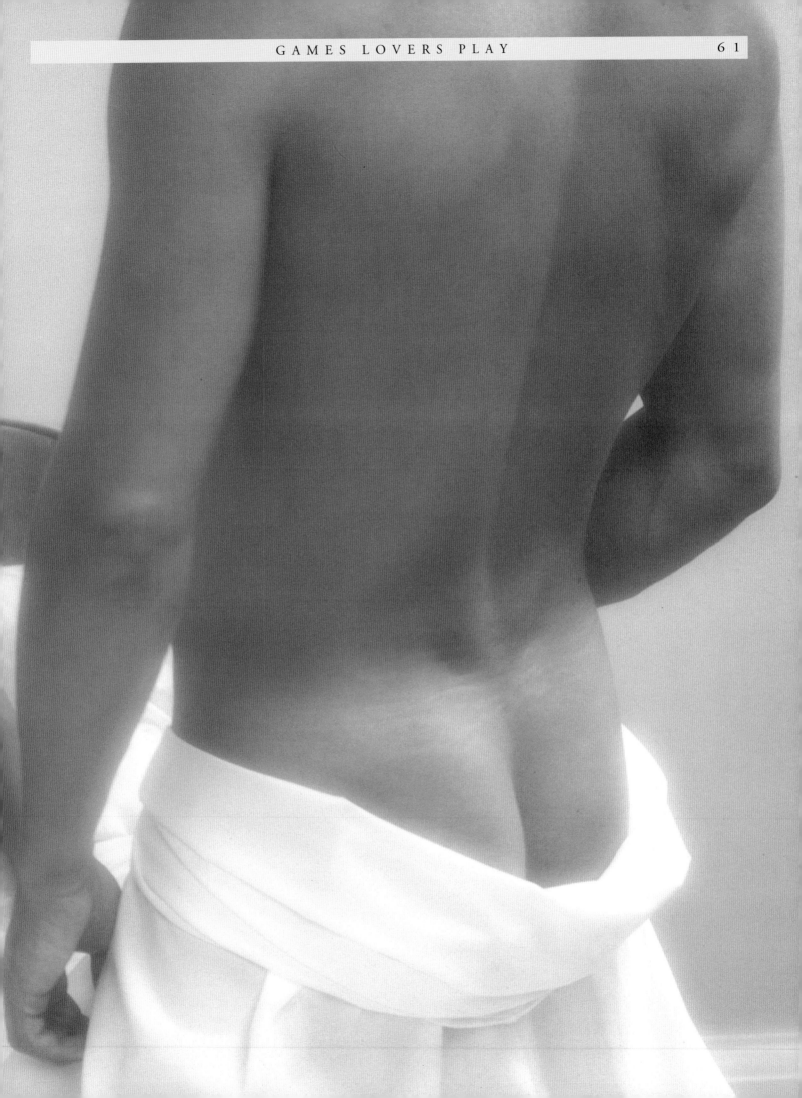

The Wild Wet

Sharing a bath or showering together can be an erotic start to an evening's pleasure.

Cleanliness is next to sexiness as far as lovemaking goes. Warm water and unscented soap are all you need for this. The fresh and natural scent of a clean body is a real turn-on.

A warm bath can be one of the most conducive ways to start an evening, washing away the day's stresses and slipping into the world of sensual pleasure. Add a splash of foam bath under a running tap, some essential oil just as you get in or even a dash of your favourite scent. When your partner joins you, the fun starts here.

The bathtub is an ideal place for long-drawn-out sex games. Enjoy the feeling of water buoying you up and watch your lover's breasts or balls floating gently. Caress

them with soapy hands. Explore the different textures against your skin and your lover's – stroke each other with sponges, brushes, cloths, the slipperiness of soap and the froth of shower gels. Massage each

other's shoulders with soapy fingers, then move on to feet, thighs and buttocks.

Sex in the shower can be sensuously erotic. Dodging water in your face as you kiss and linking up before too much soapy water gets inside just adds to the excitement. If there are solid walls to wedge against, she'll be able to get her legs around his waist. Just watch out for glass screens and treat yourselves to a non-slip mat.

Why not spill over onto the bathroom floor, with a thick towel to lie on? Use a shower gel that makes masses of lather and cover yourselves in this creamy foam. While the man lies back on the floor, the woman can lie on top and slither all over him, skating on a film of soap suds.

Toys for Boys & Girls

Vibrators and other sex toys can add a frisson of excitement.

Vibration is a very erotic feeling, which is why there are so many jokes about people's affection for their washing machines or motorbikes.

So it's not surprising that vibrators are the most popular sex toy. Either partner may enjoy lying back and being stimulated, or they may want to do it for themselves while their partner looks on. Though some women like to feel a vibrator inside them, others prefer to rub it gently around the outside or even on other parts of their bodies.

This can be just as enjoyable for a man, so try circling it around the edge of his penis and testicles for a start, or behind the testicles to stroke along his perineum.

Though old-style sex shops were depressing places, these days big cities have shops that anyone could enjoy a look in, even if more for a joke than a serious purchase. You might be surprised at what

Vibrators have moved with the times. They're available in every texture you could think of, and quite a few you wouldn't; ribbed, frilled, coiled, studded, you name it. They can look like bits of anonymous plastic, realistic penises with or without foreskin, tongues, fingers, eggs or oversized lipsticks.

You can get ones that thrust, bend, make sexy groans, spurt liquid and even glow in the dark! They're not called 'sex toys' for nothing – you're as likely to end up in fits of laughter as in erotic ecstasy, but that's a liberating feeling too.

you find. Flavoured creams and oils are popular, alongside the sexy underwear (for men too), condoms and equipment. You can buy all these by mail order (ensure you buy from a reputable catalogue) though you'll get the best idea of what you like by shopping in person.

While you're shopping, have a look at things like plain or studded balls that women can hold inside their vaginas. These can give you a sexy feeling while you walk around, strengthening your grip at the same time – you wouldn't want to drop one of these in the supermarket!

Penis rings are meant to help a man keep his erection longer, and you can buy fearsome-looking ones that have a studded extension to massage the clitoris at the same time. This wouldn't work for the many women who don't like direct pressure on the clitoris, but is worth a try if you're both feeling adventurous.

Dressing-Up Games

Be someone else, in another time and place. Close the door on everyday reality and try out a new persona.

Skin is our biggest erogenous zone. No wonder so many kinds of clothes have turned us on over the centuries. The slither of silk and the slight scratchiness of lace are classics. With leather, it's the smell and sound too, and how it looks.

Some clothing is meant purely for looking at. It's usually worn by women to excite men, which in turn can give the woman a thrill. Corsets, stockings and high heels are prime examples – also anything that laces up or has a slightly restrictive effect.

Women were glad to throw these irritating garments in the dustbin of history, but used as sex toys they add a slightly kinky edge which is a turn-on in itself.

Men can do the same for their partners. The most enlightened woman may secretly thrill to a man in riding boots or tight jeans … ask and find out. Uniforms do it for some people, so if your partner dreams of making it with a fireman or a French maid, why not dress to oblige? Your sex appeal will instantly increase and it may have just as much effect on both of you, since knowing you look sexy is a very erotic feeling. Some couples buy or make entire wardrobes to play with.

As with sex toys, there's a funny side to all this that can add to its sexiness rather than detracting from it. Sex doesn't always have to be deadly serious. In fact, something that's both playful and erotic can cause a sense of physical release that intensifies sexual pleasure.

Extreme versions of everyday clothes can have a similar effect, for example if they're very tight or low-cut – our sexual instincts aren't usually very subtle. You might not want to go to work looking like a stripper or a biker, but at home is the place you can be anyone you like.

Wearing things you find sexy will excite your partner too. Ask what he or she would like to see you in. Buy clothes for your lover as well as for yourself. Don't feel you're being demeaned if your lover wants you to dress in high heels and sequins or a football strip – and don't feel your real self is being rejected.

Sex is an anarchist that doesn't care a damn about the real world, so play with it and enjoy it in safe and loving ways.

Masks have a place of their own in dressing up. Something happens when you put on a mask that changes everything.

When your face is hidden you can be a different person, free of the inhibitions you might feel as your real self. It can have the same effect on the person looking at you.

Use this to play out games and fantasies, as long as you're safe in the knowledge that you can stop the game instantly by taking the mask off.

Your Fantasy Life

Using the power of imagination to enrich your erotic pleasure, let your day dreams roam to the far shores of sensuality.

Imagination is one of the highest human achievements – though we don't always have to use it for the most high-minded purposes. We have so much of it that it spills over into our everyday existence to enrich our day dreams and our sex lives.

In our fantasies we can be anyone in any situation in the world, doing whatever we like with no guilt or consequences. In our fantasies, other people do exactly as we secretly wish.

Fantasies aren't necessary the sex life we'd like to have, even in our dreams. They can be unsettling and even frightening. The important thing is that they exist only in our heads, perhaps to be shared with a lover, perhaps not. Even rough fantasies, or things we don't want to admit to, aren't harmful in themselves. They're only dangerous if we let them leak out into reality – or if someone takes them too seriously.

The fact that some women, for example, have 'rape' fantasies doesn't mean they actually want to get battered and terrorized. They're enjoying a pretend scenario in which they don't have to take any responsibility for their sexual pleasure. In a secret fantasy they can switch it off at any moment they like, because the person who's having the fantasy has all the power. It's the same with daydreams of overpowering someone else – fine as long as you don't actually try it on someone who's not playing.

If you're constantly fantasizing about someone other than your lover, your relationship is probably in trouble (unless it's a true fantasy figure like an actor or singer). Why not try something your real partner can join in? Or imagine your partner in the same exciting role as the person in your fantasy?

Fantasies are part of your private inner world, and don't have to be shared. But, if you like, they can add a whole new dimension to your real sex life.

When you're both feeling relaxed and close, try telling your lover about one of your secret daydreams, starting with something un-shocking and gauging their reaction.

Not everyone is going to turn on to the same things, no matter how compatible you are in other ways, and if either of you really

dislikes the other's fantasy you probably won't have much fun sharing it. So try to find some that work for both of you.

Just talking about each other's fantasies can heighten arousal, especially if you quote

one of your partner's favourite scenarios back to them while you're making love: 'I've found you lying asleep on the beach … I'm longing to touch you … You don't wake up when I run my hand up your thigh …'

The Wild Side

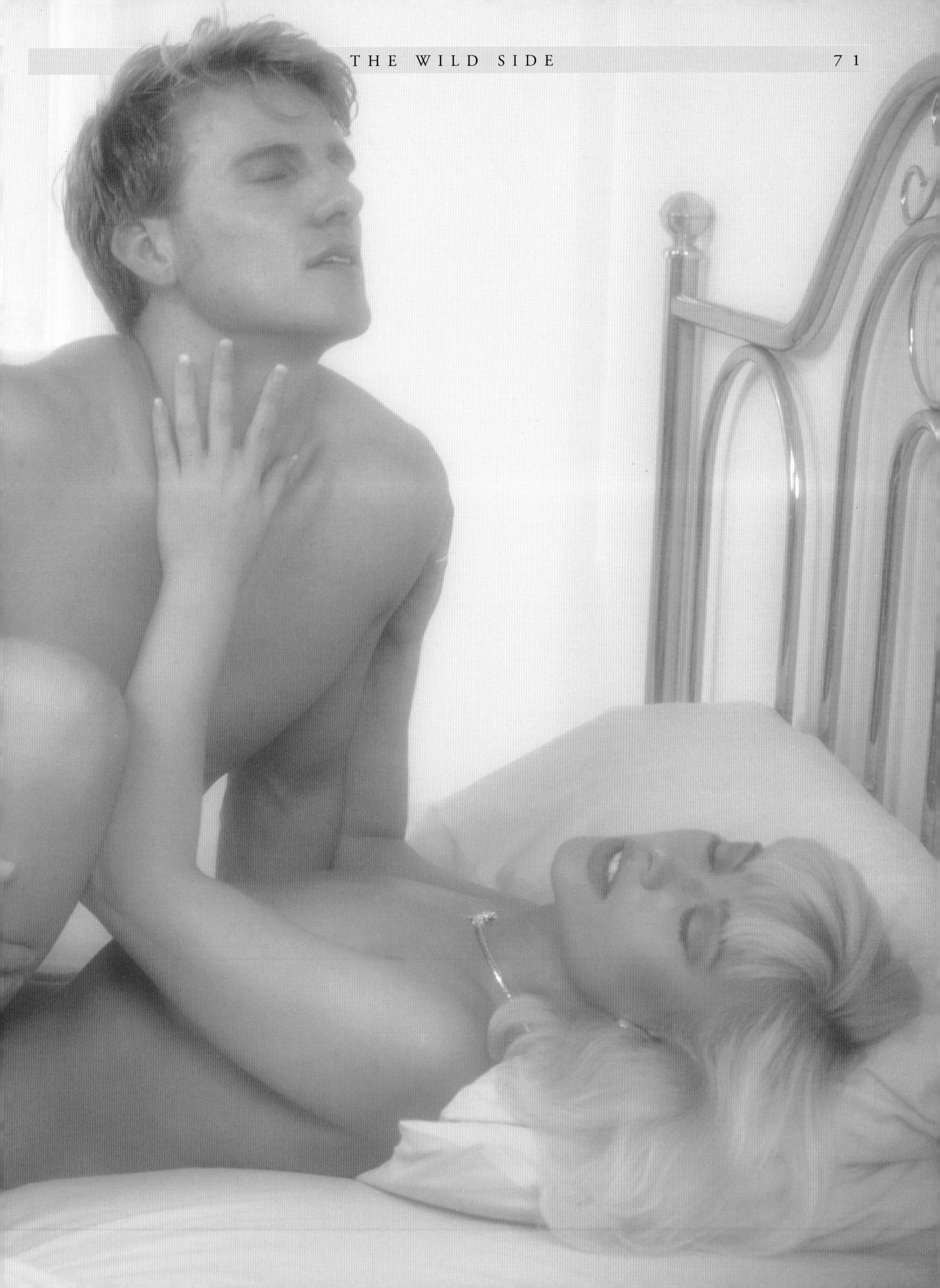

Bondage & Domination

Tying down your lover may bring out a mischievous spirit that arouses both of you. And being tied down can have a startling effect in freeing you from old inhibitions.

Most of us have grown up with so many inhibitions about sex, it's no wonder they're hard to escape when we're finally allowed to do it. Some people can't truly let go unless they're literally tied down – able to imagine they have no control over events.

For others, tying their partner (or being tied) to the bed is just another play scenario with the added edge of breaking a bit of a taboo. For people who thresh around a lot during sex, adding resistance is an easy way to a faster and more powerful orgasm. If

you have to cling to the bedhead to stop yourself taking off, tying your wrists and ankles allows you to let go.

Bondage is also about fantasies of dominating or being dominated. It's fine if one of you likes playing each part – as long as this doesn't spill over into a domineering/subservient relationship in real life – or if you both like taking turns.

For some couples, the fantasy includes wrestling, struggling, being held down and threatened or spanked. It's just another

example of the wild beast Sex breaking out and thumbing its nose at convention. As long as no one is getting genuinely hurt and you're both enjoying it, do what you like.

Don't feel your partner doesn't trust you, though, if he or she is reluctant to be held down or tied up. For some people this causes such a gut feeling of claustrophobia, totally unrelated to their feelings for you, that it would instantly kill all sexual arousal.

If you do play this game, you can buy handcuffs or leather wrist and ankle restraints from sex shops. But silk scarves have an erotic feel of their own, and you can tie them in such a way that the tied partner can choose to slip out of them when they want.

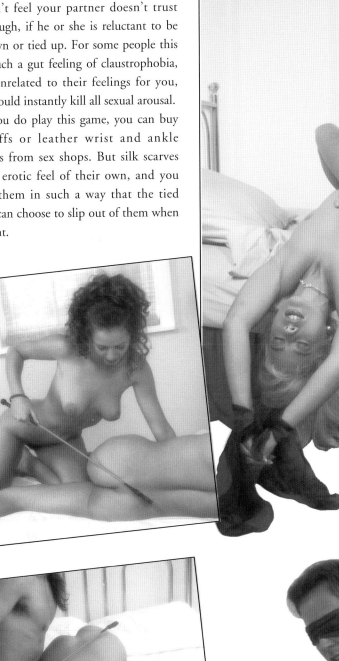

Pressing The Panic Button

Sex is surrounded by noises, cries, writhing and sometimes bites or light blows. So you wouldn't always know if your partner was having a mind-blowing orgasm or finding it difficult to breathe!

All the more so if one of you is tied up or being held down. Cries of 'No!' or 'Stop!' or even 'Help!' can be part of a fantasy scenario.

So you need a panic signal that means 'Stop right now' – and make sure both of you know this has to be respected at once, every time. This could be a word you've agreed on, for example 'Panic' or 'Release'. Or two slaps on the bed or floor – useful if your voice is muffled in the pillows. It's vital to know your partner will stop or rescue you instantly on this signal.

Creating trust allows both of you to try adventures that could otherwise be a bit scary. Needless to say, don't break this rule or do anything to your partner without their consent. At the very least, it will stop them ever trusting you again. And don't let your partner tie you down if you don't trust them – though in that case you would probably be far better off without them altogether.

Outdoor Adventures

Let the sun and air play over your skin, waking up your senses for a long afternoon of love in the grass.

There's something uniquely sensual about a sunny day. Lying on a beach or in long grass is one physical pleasure that readily brings others to mind and, if you're not likely to be stopped, why not go ahead?

A woodland setting is ideal. Naked among the trees you can start to feel like a nature spirit, unbounded by foolish mortal inhibitions. A coat or blanket to roll on saves you from painful interruptions by insects or prickly grass. And the sun on your skin invites you to surrender to sensual pleasure.

If there's no countryside within reach, remember that even an urban garden offers space and privacy on a dark, balmy summer's night. Muffling your sighs and giggles just adds to the excitement of the moment.

A secluded beach is another perfect spot, since making love in the water allows you to try many of the more complicated

or difficult positions without gravity interfering. It's simplicity itself for a woman to twine her legs around her lover's waist. You can even float blissfully while your lover tongues your tenderest parts.

When making love in water, there's the problem of water washing natural lubrication away of course, but you can either throw yourself down on the shore or make up for it with lashings of lubricating jelly. When you're lying together at the water's edge after you've made love, the little rippling waves feel like an extension of your own orgasm.

Secret Sex in Public

Suppose you slipped off your long coat and were naked underneath, glimmering under the street light …

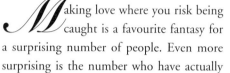

*M*aking love where you risk being caught is a favourite fantasy for a surprising number of people. Even more surprising is the number who have actually tried it. Few manage to go all the way unless they've found a temporarily private spot – the spare bedroom with a party raging all around, a dense patch

of trees in a park, even a high-speed grab in a cavernous doorway, to the sound of wild muffled giggles. But many more have shared secret sex games with an oblivious audience.

Darkness is useful, as in cinemas. Crowds can help rather than hinder, since they provide an excuse to press against each other. In some places you can openly cling to each other, like on motorbikes or jolting, overcrowded trains.

Favourite ploys include going out with only sexy underwear (or nothing) under your coat – a variation involves not telling your lover about this till you're out together, but you'd better be sure they won't blow a

fuse when they find out. The trouble is, it's quite easy to spot when couples are doing this, even when they clearly think they're being really secretive – so be subtle and this will add to the anticipation.

The point of this game is keeping it a secret, so don't be obvious enough to get arrested. But you can play with subtle signals, like wearing a dab of the scented oil you use for an intimate massage on an evening out, or slipping a trigger word that no one else would recognize from your favourite fantasy into your conversation when you're shopping together – anything that will turn your lover's thoughts to your body.

Pretend you've never met before and let your lover pick you up in a bar or at a bus stop. Play as if it's real, trying your most seductive looks and lines, maybe both playing other characters. Go home together, still playing your roles.

❧

Try to stay as this other person – who may be more uninhibited or more sensual than your usual self – while you make love. See how you feel in this different role. Come back to your real selves and talk about it before you go to sleep.

A Sense of Adventure

The quality of a sexual experience may be enhanced with a little imagination. Variations of your favourite positions could be wildly exciting and bring a satisfying new dimension to your love life.

Take It To The Limit

Share your secret sexual desires and take it in turns to suggest different positions and techniques. Act out your fantasies and discover the infinite variations made possible by imaginative lovers.

Athletic Positions

The more advanced positions may demand a high degree of suppleness from an adventurous couple, but upside-down positions can result in an intense climax, particularly when the whole body is involved in maintaining the rhythm.

Dangersex

Taking risks is a thrill that sharpens sexual excitement. Don't fight the urge – use your imagination to enjoy it and survive.

AIDS isn't the only way sex can kill you. People have found some inventive ways, including cutting off the blood supply to their brains in the hope of heightening and prolonging an orgasm.

Why are we so attracted to danger? Even children love scary cartoons, gruesome fairy tales and games of hiding and stalking. As teenagers we graduate to stomach-churning fairground rides, horror films and in some cases reckless driving – not a particularly bright idea if you want to enjoy the rest of your life.

Most of us survive to find safer ways of sublimating our danger urge. But some never really grow out of flirting with death. Refusing to use condoms isn't the only way you could kill yourself through sex.

Using drugs to heighten an orgasm can have fatal effects, and a number of accidental deaths by hanging or suffocation have been caused by people trying to cut off the blood supply to their brain while masturbating. To heighten sensations, use one of the inverted positions for sex, or try lying on the bed with your head over the edge.

Don't get talked into anything that causes serious pain or real humiliation (sado-masochism). Sex games like bondage and play-fighting let people work off some aggression harmlessly, but if your (or your lover's) aggression takes a more frightening form, you should seek professional help at once. Anal intercourse can pass on AIDS, and cause internal injuries.

If you wish to have sex in a car, drive off the road and stop. On a motorbike, keep the engine running in neutral if you like (though not in a garage, where it could become an imaginative double suicide) but put the stand down and mind the exhaust!

In fact, if dangersex attracts you, enjoy it through fantasies, role playing or watching it in action films.

Making It Easy

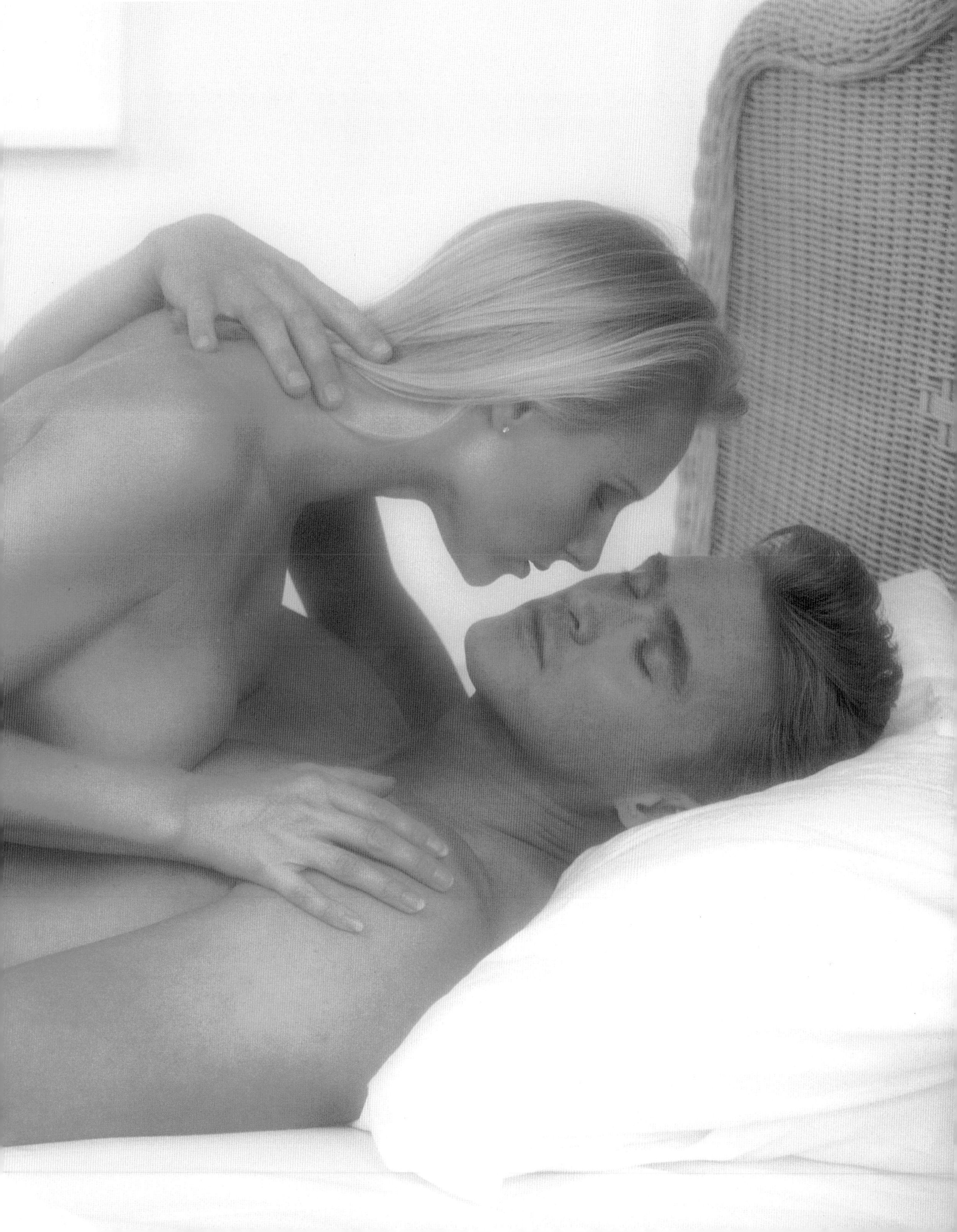

Sensual Massage

*This loving touch is the perfect way to start an evening.
But don't stop there it's also the most sensuous way of
exploring your lover's body.*

Massage has to be the world's most adaptable health treatment – since that was its original function. As well as easing the pain of knotted muscles it soothes away stress – the biggest passion-killer of the modern age.

Touch is the body's most erotic sense. Blindfold yourselves, put in ear plugs and explore the warmth and contours and textures of each other's body – all except genitals, this time, so you don't lose the chance of finding all the other erogenous zones. Try to sense where your partner is feeling most pleasure. Afterwards, tell each other what you liked best. Explore again, with sight and sound this time. Another time, continue the blindfold exploration with no holds barred, over your whole bodies.

Buy some scented oil you both like – sandalwood and patchouli have a musky aroma that many people find erotic, but there are dozens of others to choose from. Other reputed aphrodisiacs include cardamom, cedarwood, clary sage, jasmine, juniper, myrtle, neroli, rose and ylang ylang. Take it in turns to smooth a little oil into each other as you lie in a warm room on a thick towel on the floor, perhaps with incense burning.

Rub it in with long, slow, deep strokes using the flat of your hands to feel the muscle move below the skin. Knead with the pads of your fingers (not digging with fingertips). Don't press on joints or the spine, but run your thumbs deeply up the muscles beside the spine, easing out the tension they hold. Stroke the feet and gently pull the toes. Intersperse these real massage techniques with long caressing strokes the length of the body. Tease your lover by running your nails lightly down their inner arm or up their thigh.

It's worth buying a massage book or video, since there are so many techniques you can learn and use as part of your relaxed love-making. You can give a rewarding massage with just a few basic moves and a lot of time for taking pleasure.

Skin pleasures such as massage have a special role to play when your sex drive is low. Therapists advise couples to spend evenings together enjoying each other's body in every possible way except genital contact.

❧

You can imagine how the erotic tension rises as you force yourself not to go all the way. Eventually the tiny sparks of desire blaze into an inferno.

❧

But it relies on really holding yourself back. This also frequently solves men's erection anxieties, since there's no pressure on them.

Take It Easy

Love games are for everyone, regardless of age, health or ability. When sex isn't straightforward you have to use more imagination – and this always adds to the fun.

It happens to the best of us – a bike accident, a football game or one aerobics class too many and we're off our feet for a while. For some of us it's a longer-term problem, whether we're restricted by disabilities, ill health or some old injury that makes itself felt at the most inopportune moments. And then there's the psychological aspect of injuries or disability, the feeling that our body is unlovable, even ruined.

Making love with an injured or disabled partner requires a lot of sensitivity. Yet oddly enough there's an advantage too. When routine wham-bam-thank-you-ma'am sex isn't a possibility, you're forced to discover slower, more sensuous paths to pleasure. The same after an injury – love-making takes on an imaginative new dimension as we discover pleasures of the flesh that don't hurt our bones. A loving

massage not only relieves a lot of pain, it also helps anyone feel happier in their body.

Pregnancy is another time when bodily changes suggest new paths to pleasure. Women are often at their most sensuous during this time, thanks to a surge of female hormones. And with glowing skin and abundant new curves they're sexier than ever. Yet they may take some convincing that they're not fat and unappealing. The sideways-on position is easy at this time, with her lying on her back – propped up with cushions if this is more comfortable – and her man beside her. As she gets bigger and doesn't want to lie on her back, rear-entry positions are most enjoyable, either

lying on her side with her upper knee supported, kneeling forward on piles of cushions or even sitting astride a chair.

Anyone with a bad back should avoid doggy-style sex unless they're supported on plenty of cushions. Lying on your side is easiest, especially entering from behind.

Getting older can increase your capacity for sexual pleasure. Older men are less likely to suffer premature ejaculation and have more time to spend on kissing and caressing before a second erection.

Women find it easier to have orgasms as they leave their youthful anxieties behind, and lubricating jelly solves the problem if there's any dryness. But if sexual intercourse ever becomes painful, do see your doctor or go to a special clinic. Painful sex can sometimes be a sign of sexually transmitted diseases, but it is rarely serious in any way and is usually easy to treat.

Sex Problems

*There are few difficulties that can't be solved by talking,
listening and taking time for each other.*

Every man finds he can't get an erection now and then, or can't keep it up, usually because he's too tired or stressed or because he's been drinking. Drugs of all kinds including prescribed medicines can have the same effect. If it happens frequently for no apparent reason he should see his doctor for a check-up. But what often happens is that, in a vicious cycle, his anxiety about impotence makes him unable to get or keep an erection.

Learning to relax will help, as will a sympathetic partner and some imagination about trying all-body pleasures. There are many routes to sexual satisfaction and you may both enjoy these new games so much you're not too bothered about his erections – which is, of course, the best way to bring them back.

Anxiety can make love difficult for a woman too. Her muscles may knot up so tightly that he can't get in – a painful condition called vaginismus. It happens even if she isn't aware of feeling uneasy at the time and really wants to let him in.

Often she just needs more time to relax physically, since the muscle spasm is quite outside her control. It may help to try some relaxation techniques or share a soothing massage before lovemaking. If the problem persists, it may stem from a physical problem or deep-seated anxieties, so she should see her doctor and ask about counselling.

If a woman has difficulty reaching orgasm it's often simply because she needs more time to become aroused. Taking time at the early stages allows a satisfying continuation for both partners.

Loss of desire can happen in the happiest, most loving relationship. Again, it's often caused by tiredness or stress. But it can mean something wrong between you, so do talk to each other – about other problems you may be having, not just sexual ones. Listen too, rather than trying to score points. A good relationship is worth some work.

Why not set aside a day, say once a month, when you can enjoy every sexual game you like but without intercourse or oral sex? It keeps you sensitive to all the other possibilities of pleasure.

GOOD TIMING

If a man suffers from premature ejaculation – coming too quickly – some sex therapists recommend a woman-on-top position. He should tell her when he's becoming too excited, then she can lift off him and press his penis ridge with her fingers for three or four seconds. After about half a minute she can slip it back in, carefully since he may have lost some of his erection. Or she can press on his perineum for a few seconds. Young men often have hair-trigger responses, but age and experience eventually solves the problem.

If he has the problem of continuing so long they both get bored, he could try stretching the skin of his penis back tightly and holding it at the root throughout intercourse. It also helps if the woman learns to squeeze his penis tight inside her.

More Information

CONTRACEPTION

Fear about pregnancy is a big turn-off, though you don't have to worry if you're using condoms for safer sex. Seek advice from your doctor to find out the most suitable form of contraception for you and your partner.

The Pill Still the commonest form of contraception. Like any drug, it brings risks as well as benefits and it's important to take advice from your doctor to ensure that it is suitable for you. It is a reliable contraceptive if you follow the instructions carefully.

Contraceptive Injections You don't have to remember to take a pill every day, but you're getting a large dose of drug, so this method may not be suitable for everyone.

Implants Another easy option for the forgetful, but they can be painful and difficult to remove.

Intrauterine Device (IUD or coil) Modern technology has improved these. Once it's in you don't have to think about it. If a coil starts hurting, though, get back to your doctor fast to avoid pelvic inflammatory disease which may possibly cause infertility.

(Dutch) Cap or Diaphragm A springy little dome-shaped device that can cause either hilarity or deathly embarrassment if it shoots out while you're trying to put it in. You do have to remember to use it every time and you're advised to add spermicidal cream or gel, which makes it even slipperier. Harmless and effective, it's one of the world's oldest forms of contraception.

Cervical Cap A smaller, squashier version of the diaphragm, easier to insert because it doesn't have a springy rim. Like the diaphragm, it may offer protection against some infections too (but not against AIDS).

The Condom Back in favour thanks to its effectiveness against sexually transmitted diseases, the condom is reliable as long as you remember to use one every time.

Female Condoms Bulky and inconvenient till you get used to them, but probably as effective as the male condom and an excellent protection against disease.

Sterilization Only if you're positive you don't ever want any more children. It can sometimes be reversed, but this can't be guaranteed. The man's operation is simpler than the woman's.

SAFE AND SEXY

You could spend a whole lifetime discovering the pleasures of the flesh, so don't risk throwing it all away.

Sexually transmitted diseases are very sociable and love getting around. Any exchange of bodily fluids could pass on the virus that causes AIDS, and, apart from junkies sharing needles (and being in poor health to fight off infections) that's usually through genital or mouth-to-genital contact. The more partners you have the more you increase your risk. Anal sex is especially risky, and can cause internal injuries too.

There are only two forms of (pretty much) safe sex. You can either use a condom – male or female version – every time. Or you can enjoy the wealth of erotic pleasures that don't involve penis or vagina meeting anything else: making out, tangling together with clothes on – all those wonderful high-school delights we tend to forget in the adult world.

But monogamy is the only really safe route. Use these precautions till you've been together six months and then, if neither of you has had unprotected sex with anyone else in that time, you can go to a clinic for AIDS tests. Don't go to your own doctor in case nosy insurance companies or future employers want to see your medical records.

FURTHER READING

The New Joy of Sex
by Alex Comfort,
Mitchell Beazley 1994.
How to Improve Your Sex Life
by Dr David Delvin,
Hodder & Stoughton 1983.
The Tao of Love and Sex: the ancient Chinese way to ecstasy
by Jolan Chang,
Wildwood 1977, Gower 1995.
Erotic Massage
by Janet Wright,
Parragon 1997.